CHOOSING DEMOCRACY

How Has Democracy Evolved?

Rebecca Sjonger

CRABTREE
PUBLISHING COMPANY
WWW.CRABTREEBOOKS.COM

CRABTREE
PUBLISHING COMPANY
WWW.CRABTREEBOOKS.COM

Author: Rebecca Sjonger
Series research and development: Janine Deschenes
Editors: Ellen Rodger, Janine Deschenes
Proofreader: Wendy Scavuzzo
Design and photo research: Katherine Berti
Print and production coordinator: Katherine Berti

Dedicated by Rebecca Sjonger:
For my favorite Knappett
(you know who you are)

Front cover: *Washington Rallying the Troops at Monmouth* is an 1856 painting by Emanuel Leutze. It shows an idealized, or not quite real, vision of George Washington leading the Continental Army against the British Army in a battle during the American Revolutionary War (1775-1783). The war led to an independent and democratic United States of America.

Image credits:
AfriPics: Bernie Olbrich: p. 35 (bottom)
Alamy Stock Photo
CPA Media Pte Ltd: p. 8
Ian Pilbeam: p. 12 (bottom)
Lake Erie Maps and Prints: p. 4 (left)
Lakeview Images: p. 17
Reuters: p. 36 (bottom)
The Picture Art Collection: p. 9
Alexander Turnbull Library, Wellington, New Zealand: Photograph of an engraving showing women going to the poll at Devonport, 1893. Making New Zealand: Negatives and prints from the Making New Zealand Centennial collection. Ref: MNZ-2834-1/4-F. /records/22630436: p. 30 (top)
Government of Canada: p 23 (bottom)
Photo by Adam Scotti, Permission granted by the Office of the Prime Minister, © Her Majesty the Queen in Right of Canada, 2021: p. 5
Library of Congress: p. 31 (bottom)
National Archives: p. 19
New York Public Library: Johnston's Studio (Columbia, SC) (photographer): p. 28
Shutterstock
360b: p. 39 (bottom right)
Alessia Pierdomenico: p. 36 (top)
Art Babych: p. 43 (bottom left)
Cavan-Images: p 13 (center right)
coloursinmylife: p. 38
Jess Pomponio: p. 45
John Gress Media In: p. 42 (bottom)
MidoSemsem: p. 37 (top right)
Nuno21: p. 43 (bottom center)
Phil Pasquini: p. 43 (top)
photocosmos1: p. 43 (bottom right)
R. Bociaga: p. 39 (top)
spatuletail: p. 7 (center right)
United Nations: p. 40 (top)
Wikimedia Commons
Arthur C. Michael (d. 1945): p. 14 (top left)
Biblioteca del Congreso Nacional—Chile: p. 32
catalog.archives.gov/id/196283: p. 30 (bottom)
Chiloa: p. 22 (bottom)
Collections.chateauversailles.fr/#ab1256a3-7143-43d9-b317-3bb58e03a1d2: p. 21 (bottom)
Coyau: p. 11 (top)
Cyril Jessop: p. 29
Domenick D'Andrea: p. 1
Edinburgh Geographical Institute; J. G. Bartholomew and Sons: p. 34 (bottom left)
Edward Linley Sambourne (1844–1910): p. 35 (top)
ELEL09: p. 37 (bottom left)
Elliott && Fry: p. 34 (bottom right)
Emanuel Leutze, Doe Memorial Library, Smithsonian Art Inventory Catalog, IAP 71061327 Monmouth County Historical Association American Heritage—www.americanrevolution.com, www.lib.berkeley.edu, Provenance: front cover
Gryffindor: p. 21 (top)
HgEx40kfRvtojQ at Google Arts & Culture: p. 15 (center right)
Hugo van Gelderen / Anefo: p. 31 (top)
L'Histoire par l'image: p. 6
Library of Congress: p. 27 (both)
Makaristos: p. 4 (right)
Malala Yousafzai Education for girls: p. 41 (bottom)
Original authors were the barons and King John of England. Uploaded by Earthsound: p. 14–15 (bottom)
Original, Second Continental Congress, reproduction, William Stone: p. 18 (bottom)
Presidenza della Repubblica: p. 37 (bottom center)
Prioryman: p. 11 (bottom)
Raffaele Giannetti: p. 10 (bottom)
Ramón Sagredo: p. 33 (top)
PuebloUnited: p. 33 (bottom right)
Rob984: p. 23 (top)
Scottish National Gallery: p. 16
The AMICA Libra: p. 22 (top)
US Capitol: p. 26
White House Historical Association: p. 11 (center right)
www.kremlin.ru Presidential Press and Information Office: p. 37 (bottom right)
Yale University Art Gallery: p. 18 (top)
All other images from Shutterstock

Crabtree Publishing Company
www.crabtreebooks.com **1-800-387-7650**

Printed in the U.S.A./072022/CG20220201

Published in Canada
Crabtree Publishing
616 Welland Ave.
St. Catharines, Ontario
L2M 5V6

Published in the United States
Crabtree Publishing
347 Fifth Ave
Suite 1402-145
New York, NY 10016

Library and Archives Canada Cataloguing in Publication
Available at the Library and Archives Canada

Library of Congress Cataloging-in-Publication Data
Available at the Library of Congress

Hardcover: 9781039663329 Paperback: 9781039663817
Ebook (pdf): 9781039668249 Epub: 9781039685642
Read-along: 9781039686137 Audio book: 9781039668737

Contents

Introduction

In 1776, the Thirteen Colonies declared independence from Great Britain. They were the original United States of America. Most of the citizens of this new country did not want to be ruled by distant royalty. Instead, they crafted their own laws and civic duties **that reflected their beliefs in freedom and equality.**

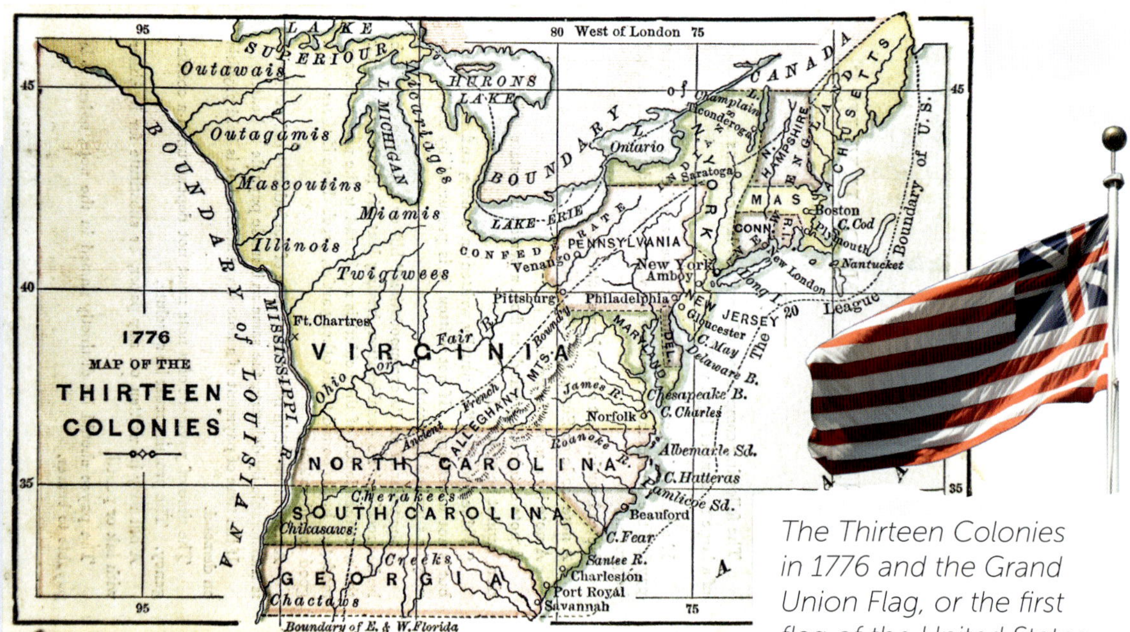

The Thirteen Colonies in 1776 and the Grand Union Flag, or the first flag of the United States.

Rule of the People

The Founding Fathers were inspired by the democratic government of the ancient Greeks. They also borrowed from the Roman **Republic**. Its leaders were chosen to speak on behalf of the people. They learned from the Haudenosaunee Confederacy of Indigenous nations of North America, too. It showed them how different groups could unite to work toward common goals. Most importantly, the founders were inspired by the ideas of individual freedom that came out of the **Age of Enlightenment**. The Age of Enlightenment was an era during the 1600s and 1700s when **philosophers** and thinkers in Europe began questioning the traditional authority of the kings and queens who ruled them. These ideals helped the United States form a republic and become the world's longest-running democracy.

Democratic Government

This book looks at how democracy developed over time, especially in the United States and Canada. But what is democracy? The example of early America shows that it has more than one meaning. For instance, it is a kind of government. A democratic government serves its citizens instead of itself. This may be in a country or a smaller area, such as a state, province, region, or city. Even schools can have their own governments. In representative democracies, voters choose who speaks and acts for them. A government is a political system. Systems have many parts that work together to meet common goals. In a government, this includes laws as well as the people who make them and put them into action.

Democratic Processes

Democracy also describes processes used by governments and other groups. A process is a set of steps taken to meet a certain goal. It can be simple or complex. Voting is one of the most important processes. The winning person or plan is chosen by the **majority** of voters. The **minority** are still heard and protected in democracies. Making decisions this way is democratic because it upholds certain core values.

In Canada, the federal government is a democractically elected parliament. Here, Prime Minister Justin Trudeau speaks after a government swearing-in ceremony in 2021.

Principles

Values or goals held by a society are also part of democracy. A liberal democracy is the form of government based on the values and principals of **liberalism**. These principals were developed during the Age of Enlightenment when people were dissatisfied with being ruled by monarchies, nobles, and the church. The political ideas that came from the Age of Enlightenment included the belief that each man (later, each human) had the right to life, liberty, and property, and that governments had no right to deny or violate these **rights**. The democratic principles of fairness and accountability came from these liberal ideas. In addition, citizens are all free to make their own choices as long as they pose no harm to others. Members of a liberal democratic society are expected to act together for the common good. The rights of citizens are protected. People have many freedoms. They can choose where they live and travel, which jobs they work at, who they meet with, and how they take part in society. In a well-functioning liberal democracy, the roles of the government, the military, police, and other leaders are limited. This helps prevent abuse of power. People also do not lose their rights and freedoms as governments change.

The Age of Enlightenment is sometimes known as the Age of Reason because it was an era that encouraged thinking, and science was emerging over superstition.

Global Forms of Government

Full democracies uphold democratic processes and principles. Flawed democracies face issues such as **corrupt** leaders or citizens not taking part. Some countries call themselves democracies, but they are not. Many of them are autocracies. In an autocracy, one person or a small group holds onto power. They use force to stop anyone who opposes them. In a military dictatorship, armed forces control the government. An absolute monarchy is also an autocracy. The ruler has total control over their subjects. Monarchies are led by the head of a royal family. They often inherit their position. Absolute monarchies, military dictatorships, and other governments are authoritarian. They have total control over citizens, who do not have many rights or freedoms.

Defining Democracy

A list of common terms

Citizen A person who is legally recognized to have the privileges of those who were born in or live in a particular place

Constitution The foundational laws that guide a country

Election A vote in which someone is chosen to hold a certain position

Independence The state of being free and not under outside control

Parliament An assembly of representatives elected to serve

Representative democracy
A government that is chosen by citizens who vote for leaders to represent them

Republic A representative government that is not led by a monarch

Rights The basic freedoms and privileges that every human is born with

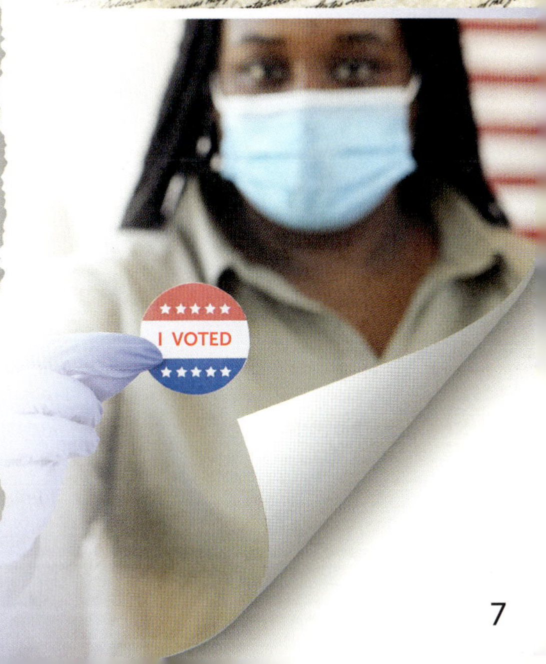

CHAPTER 1

Origins of Democracy

About 2,500 years ago, a Greek leader named Cleisthenes created *demokratia*. This new political system combined *demos* (the people) and *kratos* (power). It was an early form of democracy used in the city-state of Athens.

Cleisthenes

A city-state is an independent city and surrounding area that governs itself. Athens had a direct democracy, which means male citizens over the age of 20 debated and made decisions together. When needed, they voted. Decisions were made by majority rule.

Athenian Assembly

Equality is at the heart of modern democracy. However, the Athenian assembly was only for male citizens. They had to be aged 20 years or older. Women and people who were enslaved were not represented. The members of the assembly met on a hilltop called the Pnyx about 40 times a year. The men were expected to be informed about issues that affected Athens. They shared their opinions and also listened to each other's points of view. These important democratic values still exist today.

Early Processes

Members of the assembly were expected to take part in government processes. Like later governments, including the United States and Canada, there were multiple **branches**. For example, the Council of 500 handled daily business. It included 50 leaders from each of the 10 Athenian tribes. The government body was formed by a lottery each year. This was meant to spread out power. In another branch, citizens were randomly selected from the assembly to act as **jurors**. They worked together to make legal decisions.

The ancient Athenian assembly was called the ekklesia.

Power Plays

Direct democracy in Athens lasted from 507 BCE to 338 BCE. It did not always run smoothly, though. Some leaders thought that democracy was too **radical**. They believed that it made Athens weaker. A variety of oligarchies seized control over the years. In an oligarchy, a small group of people from the upper **class** share power. This is a form of minority rule. Over time, Macedonia took over Greece and direct democracy faded away.

Plato

Think About It!

Plato was an ancient Greek philosopher. He described Athenian democracy as "full of variety and disorder." Do you think this describes democracy today? Why or why not?

The Roman Republic

The Roman Republic existed at around the same time as direct democracy in Athens. Rome had an early kind of representative government. Densely populated areas make direct democracy impossible. In today's representative democracies, voters from all backgrounds choose who will speak for them. The version in the ancient city-state of Rome did not act on behalf of all citizens. Starting in 509 BCE, the wealthiest and most powerful Romans began forming assemblies. Those groups made decisions for the rest of the population as they saw fit.

The first Roman emperor, Augustus Caesar, was an autocrat. He ruled the Roman Empire with an iron fist.

Adding Members

Over time, new councils with different roles were added. They included more people from lower classes—but only free, adult men. Two consuls were elected to be the heads of state each year. They ran the military and the **senate**. Rome moved away from representative government when Augustus Caesar took power in 27 BCE.

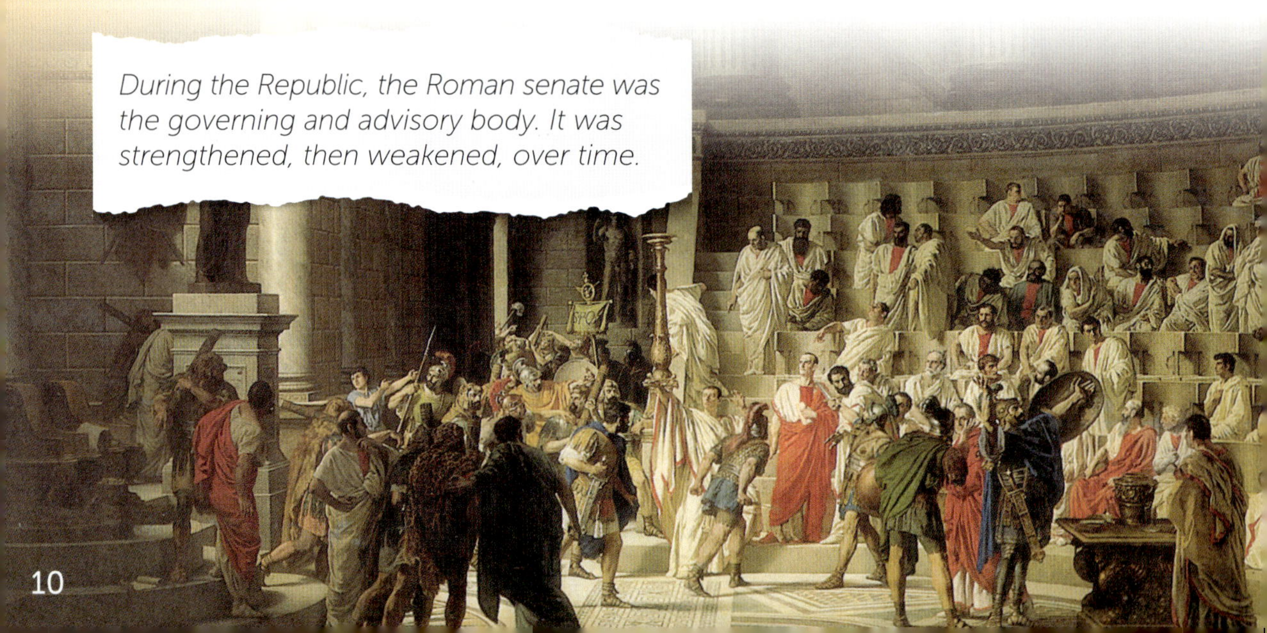

During the Republic, the Roman senate was the governing and advisory body. It was strengthened, then weakened, over time.

Cyrus the Great

Case Study

The Cyrus Cylinder

In contrast to the Greeks and Romans, the first king of ancient Persia (present-day Iran) believed that enslaved people had rights. Cyrus the Great gained control of Babylon (present-day Iraq) in 539 BCE. He freed the enslaved people there. King Cyrus declared that people from different racial backgrounds were equal. He also protected religious freedoms. These decrees, or royal orders, were written on a clay cylinder. It was discovered by an archaeologist in 1879. The Cyrus Cylinder is thought to be the earliest record calling for rights for all humans. The king's life is described in an ancient book called the *Cyropaedia*. Thomas Jefferson studied it. He was influenced by Cyrus's views on democratic ideals. Jefferson was a founder of the United States and its third president.

Thomas Jefferson was also a slaveholder who could not adjust his ideals on freedom as meaning freedom for those he enslaved.

Cyrus Cylinder

Law Rock in Thingvellir National Park, Iceland. Laws were once proclaimed here.

Oldest Parliament

Althing is the world's oldest parliament. A parliament is a governing body, or legislature, that makes laws through majority rule. Althing was formed in Iceland in 930 CE. Leaders from different areas of the island met each year. They were not chosen by or accountable to the people. Instead, these leaders acted in their own interests. They gathered at Thingvellir, which comes from the Old Norse words *thing* (assembly) and *vellir* (field). They reviewed their laws and discussed new ones. Whoever was speaking stood on a rock known as Law Rock. They lost power when Norway took control of Iceland in 1262. Iceland later became part of Denmark. The Althing was reinstated as a parliament in 1874. Iceland is now a representative democracy.

Crowds gather for Tynwald Day on the Isle of Man. On this national day, or public holiday, the island's legislature meets to publicly proclaim laws. It is a tradition that has its roots in the same Law Rock proclamations as Iceland.

Longest Running Parliament

The Isle of Man's parliamentary assembly has met for more than 1,000 years. That makes it the world's longest-running parliament. Norse Vikings settled on the small island in the Irish Sea in the late 700s. Around 979, they began meeting in a field in the middle of each summer. They discussed matters that were important to everyone on the island. The annual meeting became known as Tynwald. This name comes from the same root words as Iceland's Thingvellir. The parliament of the Isle of Man became democratic in 1866. Tynwald still meets regularly today. The parliament celebrates with an outdoor ceremony on July 5 each year.

Shared Power

Another step toward democratic governments took place in 1188. Alfonso IX was the king of Spanish territories León and Galicia at the time. He gathered commoners, or ordinary people, along with nobles, or those in high social classes, and church leaders. They met in a royal council at the Basilica of San Isidoro. Together, these groups came up with the Decrees of León. The documents mapped out a system of government that improved equality. They also protected subjects from abuses of power. The council and its ideas did not create lasting change in the region. But, they did point to a future when monarchs would share their power.

Alfonso IX, king of León and Galicia.

Basilica of San Isidoro, in León, Spain

King John of England signing the Magna Carta

Magna Carta

In 1215, England was an absolute monarchy ruled by King John. English nobles and church leaders thought his **taxes** were greedy. They wanted to limit his power and improve their lives as his **subjects**. They wrote a document called the Magna Carta. This means "great charter" in Latin. A charter describes people's basic rights and privileges. The Magna Carta declared that the king must follow laws instead of doing whatever he wished. King John was forced to sign it. This led to greater legal protections for English citizens. For example, people could not be punished unless they were lawfully convicted of a crime. People's rights and freedoms increased, as well. For the first time, women and children could inherit property. The Magna Carta also ended forced marriages. As a written statement of basic rights and freedoms, it became a foundation for building future democracies.

Think About It!

In what ways did the Magna Carta change the course of history?

Petition of Right

Councils of English leaders, such as the one that limited King John's power, became parliaments. These are legislatures, or the law-making branches of government, in many democracies. In 1628, the English parliament improved the rights of English citizens again with another influential document. They created the Petition of Right. It was created in reaction to King Charles I abusing his authority. He over-taxed his subjects and forced them to give him loans. The king also upset people by having soldiers stay in private homes without permission. One of the Petition of Right's terms made sure that martial law could not be enacted during times of peace. Martial law occurs when the military takes control. It is reserved for emergencies today. A country's laws are suspended temporarily, and citizens' basic rights may be ignored. By misusing it, King Charles helped ensure that absolute monarchy in England was almost over.

King Charles I of England

CHAPTER 2

A Changing World

Charles I believed that his authority as king of England and Scotland came from God. This is called divine right. It makes it difficult to argue with anything a ruler says or does. King Charles would not accept being accountable to his subjects for his actions. He was very unpopular as a result.

The British parliament demanded to share power with him. The king refused. A **civil war** broke out between people who supported the king and those who supported the government. It lasted almost a decade. Finally, Charles I was beheaded for **treason** on January 30, 1649. These changes led to Great Britain becoming a constitutional monarchy.

King Charles' arguing with parliament, civil war, and authoritarian rule ultimately led to his public trial. He is the only British monarch to be executed for treason.

Constitutional Democracies

A monarch in this form of government shares power with elected representatives. The country's constitution outlines their roles and how they must work together. It is also a set of basic laws that protect and apply equally to all citizens. A constitution is usually a formal written record. However, Britain is among a handful of places that have an uncodified constitution. That means a collection of laws from a variety of sources steers the country instead of a single document. A constitution is a "working document," which means it can be amended, or changed. This can only be done by following strict rules, though. Democratic governments are limited by their constitutions. Leaders have enough power to do their duties but cannot abuse it for their own gain.

Think About It!

Different governments have different laws in their constitutions. How does this reflect democratic ideals?

Britain struggled with ineffective republican governments from 1649–1660. Eventually, the son of King Charles I, who had been forced to leave the country, was invited to return. He ruled as Charles II, until 1685. Over hundreds of years, Britain's parliament evolved to be more representative and democratic.

The Battle of Princeton (1777) during the American Revolution.

American Independence

British colonists living in North America were taxed like British citizens. They did not have the same representation in the government, however. They were angry that King George III ruled over them from across the ocean. Thirteen colonies—the United States—rebelled in 1775. This sparked the American Revolution. The new country approved the Declaration of Independence on July 4, 1776. This important founding document highlighted the central ideas of the new **ideology** of liberalism: the rights and freedoms of individuals. It also included the right to rise up against the tyranny of the monarchy.

Check It Out!

https://www.archives.gov/founding-docs/declaration-transcript

IN CONGRESS, JULY 4, 1776.

...nanimous Declaration of the thirteen united States of America,

The Declaration of Independence.

Founding a Country

Britain finally recognized America's independence at the end of the war in 1783. The Constitution of the United States of America was drafted in 1787. It came into effect a couple of years later. The document laid out the fundamental laws of the new nation. It is the world's oldest written constitution. The United States was then a constitutional democracy.

Federal Republic

The United States formed a federal republic. Federalism has three levels of government: national, state, and local. The national level has authority over the country. American states run themselves with their own constitutions. They also control the local level of government for towns, cities, and regions. As a republic, the United States has no monarchy. Americans chose to have a president instead of electing a political party, which is done in a parliament. Its president is both the head of state and of the government. To keep abuses of power in check, power is shared by the president and members of the House of Representatives and the Senate. These leaders are a representative government elected by the people to speak and act on their behalf.

Check It Out!

www.archives.gov/founding-docs/constitution-transcript

The U.S. Constitution famously states, "We hold these truths to be self-evident, that all men are created equal, that they are endowed by their Creator with certain unalienable Rights, that among these are Life, Liberty and the pursuit of Happiness."

Ideas and Practice

American statesman James Madison is known for drafting the Constitution and the Bill of Rights. He was influenced by liberal philosophers and writers from the Age of Enlightenment. These influences led him to ensure the protection of minority rights in the constitution and to develop the idea of separation of powers in government. This equally divides the authority of government among the three branches to help ensure checks and balances on power. Madison later became the country's fourth president, serving from 1809 to 1817. Madison recognized that **chattel slavery** was immoral, or wrong, and had a corrupting effect on the unity of the country. He supported laws allowing enslaved people to be freed by those who owned them. But Madison also owned a plantation and enslaved people. Like many founders of early American democracy, including the first president, he could not match his ideals with all of his actions. The appeal of the living he made from enslaved labor, and the economy built from it, prevented him from applying his ideas of liberty to the people he enslaved.

James Madison

George Washington became the first president of the United States of America in 1789.

Amendments

Over the centuries, American leaders have amended, or changed, the U.S. Constitution. These changes are often based on democratic ideals and processes. The first 10 amendments are collectively known as the Bill of Rights. They were all added in 1791 to protect the rights of American citizens. They were modeled in part after the British Bill of Rights. The constitution has now been amended 27 times.

The French Revolution

The American Revolutionary War sparked other fights for democracy around the world. The most significant was the French Revolution. French citizens shared British colonists' anger over being heavily taxed by monarchs. Louis XVI and Marie Antoinette, the last king and queen of France, led the country into financial ruin. In part, this was due to France supporting the Americans in their revolution. Equality between the classes and citizens' rights were also problems in France.

Louis XVI and Marie Antoinette

Slow Change

In 1789, King Louis called a meeting of religious leaders, nobles, and common people. The huge majority were commoners. They declared themselves a new National Assembly. It brought in the Declaration of the Rights of Man and of the Citizen. This document outlined democratic values for French citizens. A written constitution was introduced in 1791. King Louis was forced into a brief constitutional monarchy. The monarchy was abolished, or ended, the next year. The king and queen were later executed by guillotine. "*Liberté, égalité, fraternité*" (liberty, equality, fraternity) became France's national motto. Political upheaval continued there for many years. The country did not become a democratic republic until 1946.

The French Revolution (1789–1802) was a series of events that changed France from an absolute monarchy to a republic. One of the events that kicked off the Revolution was the Tennis Court Oath, in 1789. It marked the first time French citizens stood together to oppose the king.

Forming Canada

Some British colonies worked with the monarchy instead of revolting against its rule. In 1867, Britain passed the British North America (BNA) Act. It turned four colonies into the Dominion of Canada. This document became known as the Constitution Act, 1867. It created a parliamentary constitutional monarchy. In Canada's system, power is held by the political party that wins the most parliamentary "seats" or ridings in the House of Commons during an election. The party leader becomes prime minister, which is the head of government. The prime minister is also a member of parliament, or MP, for their own riding. The amount of influence the Crown holds in a constitutional monarchy varies. Canada controls its own laws, but the king or queen is the head of state. The monarch yields power to the country's parliament. The monarch is represented federally by a governor general and provincially by lieutenant governors.

Sir John A. Macdonald was elected Canada's first prime minister in 1867.

Independent Canada

Over time, other colonies and territories joined Canada. They formed a federal system like the United States. In the early 1980s, Prime Minister Pierre Trudeau worked with provincial leaders to patriate the constitution, or bring it to Canada. The Constitution Act, 1867, was an act of the British parliament, known at the time as the British North America Act. This would make it easier for Canada to change its own laws. The second Constitution Act was introduced in 1982. With it, Canada gained complete independence and the power to change its rules without British permission. The Canadian Charter of Rights and Freedoms was also added. It protects Canadian citizens. These important documents include rules for the Canadian government. But, there is no single written constitution. For more than 150 years, Canada has followed many of the same unwritten rules as in Britain. For example, the American constitution lists the president's powers, while the Canadian prime minister's are not set out in writing.

Pierre Trudeau

Commonwealth Countries

Countries that were formerly part of the British Empire formed a group known as the Commonwealth of Nations.

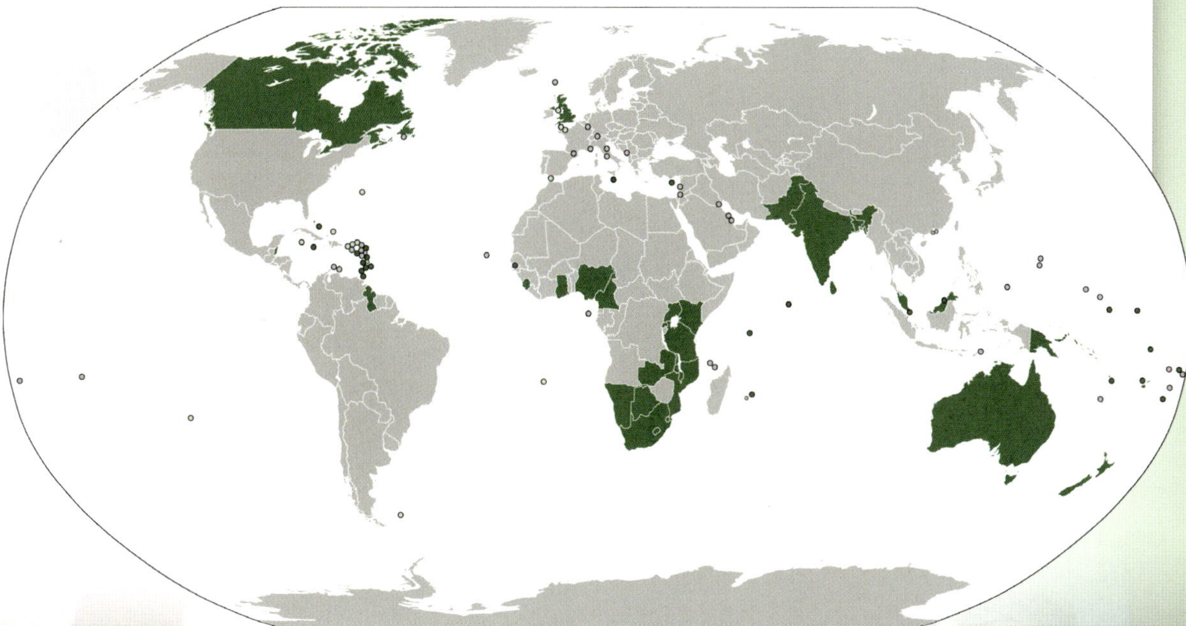

Queen Elizabeth signs Canada's Proclamation of the Constitution Act on April 17, 1982. Canada patriated its constitution but still remained a constitutional monarchy with the queen as the head of state.

World's Oldest Democracies

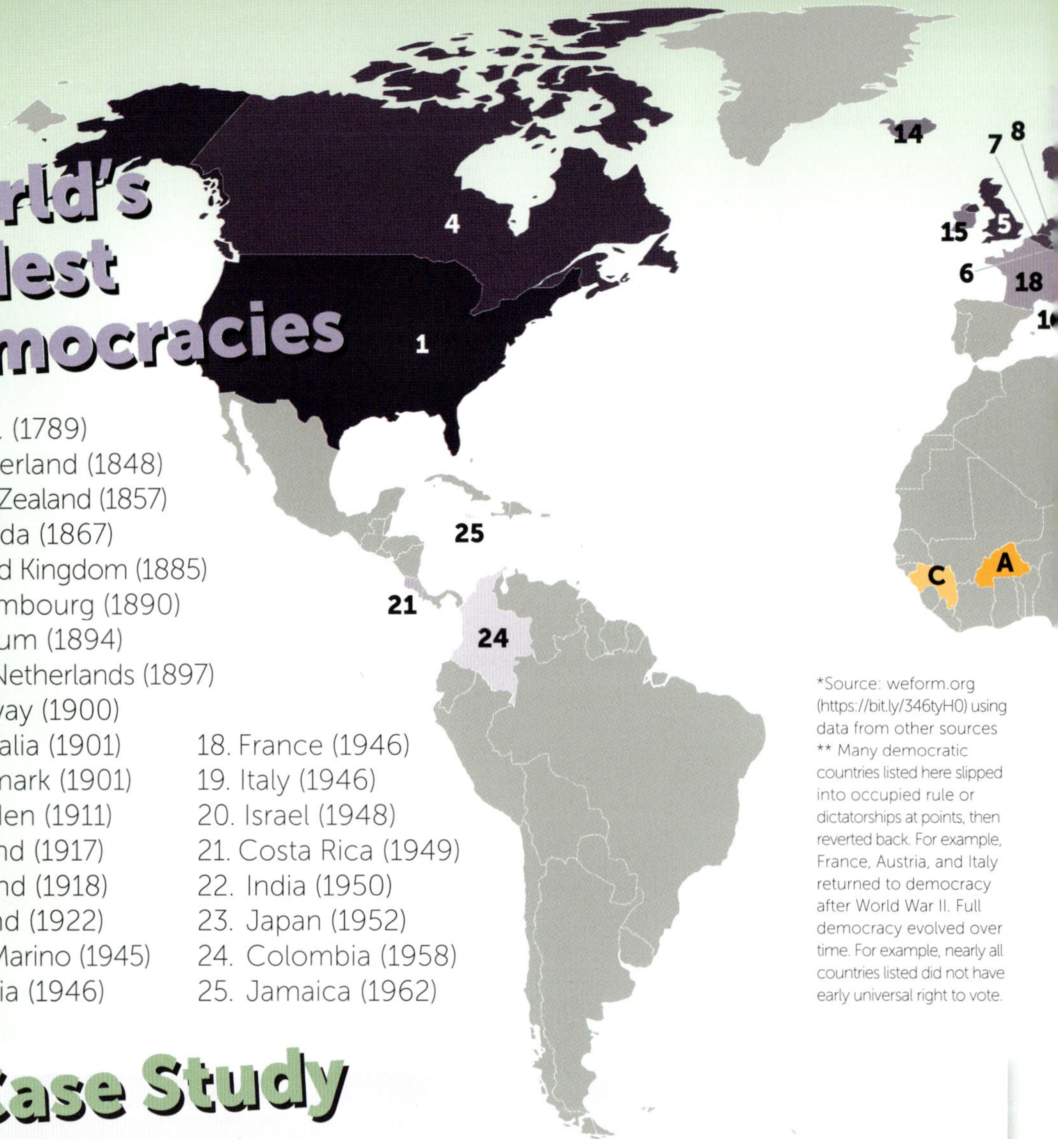

1. U.S.A. (1789)
2. Switzerland (1848)
3. New Zealand (1857)
4. Canada (1867)
5. United Kingdom (1885)
6. Luxembourg (1890)
7. Belgium (1894)
8. The Netherlands (1897)
9. Norway (1900)
10. Australia (1901)
11. Denmark (1901)
12. Sweden (1911)
13. Finland (1917)
14. Iceland (1918)
15. Ireland (1922)
16. San Marino (1945)
17. Austria (1946)
18. France (1946)
19. Italy (1946)
20. Israel (1948)
21. Costa Rica (1949)
22. India (1950)
23. Japan (1952)
24. Colombia (1958)
25. Jamaica (1962)

*Source: weform.org (https://bit.ly/346tyH0) using data from other sources
** Many democratic countries listed here slipped into occupied rule or dictatorships at points, then reverted back. For example, France, Austria, and Italy returned to democracy after World War II. Full democracy evolved over time. For example, nearly all countries listed did not have early universal right to vote.

Case Study

Secret Ballots

Voting in early democracies was not the same from place to place. In some elections, ballots were handwritten. In others, voting took place orally. Later, tickets for each political party were printed in newspapers or handed out by **campaigners**. Voters presented a candidate's ticket to a special judge on election day. In 1856, secret ballots were introduced in multiple states of Australia. This idea had been proposed before but was considered anti-democratic. Some people believed a public vote made sure that citizens worked toward the common good instead of protecting their own interests. Privacy allowed people to choose whoever they wanted. Countries around the world slowly adopted this method. Today, voters expect to be supplied with ballots on election day. Barriers prevent others from seeing who they choose.

World's Youngest Democracies

A. Burkina Faso (2015)
B. Tunisia (2011)
C. Guinea (2011)
D. Bhutan (2008)

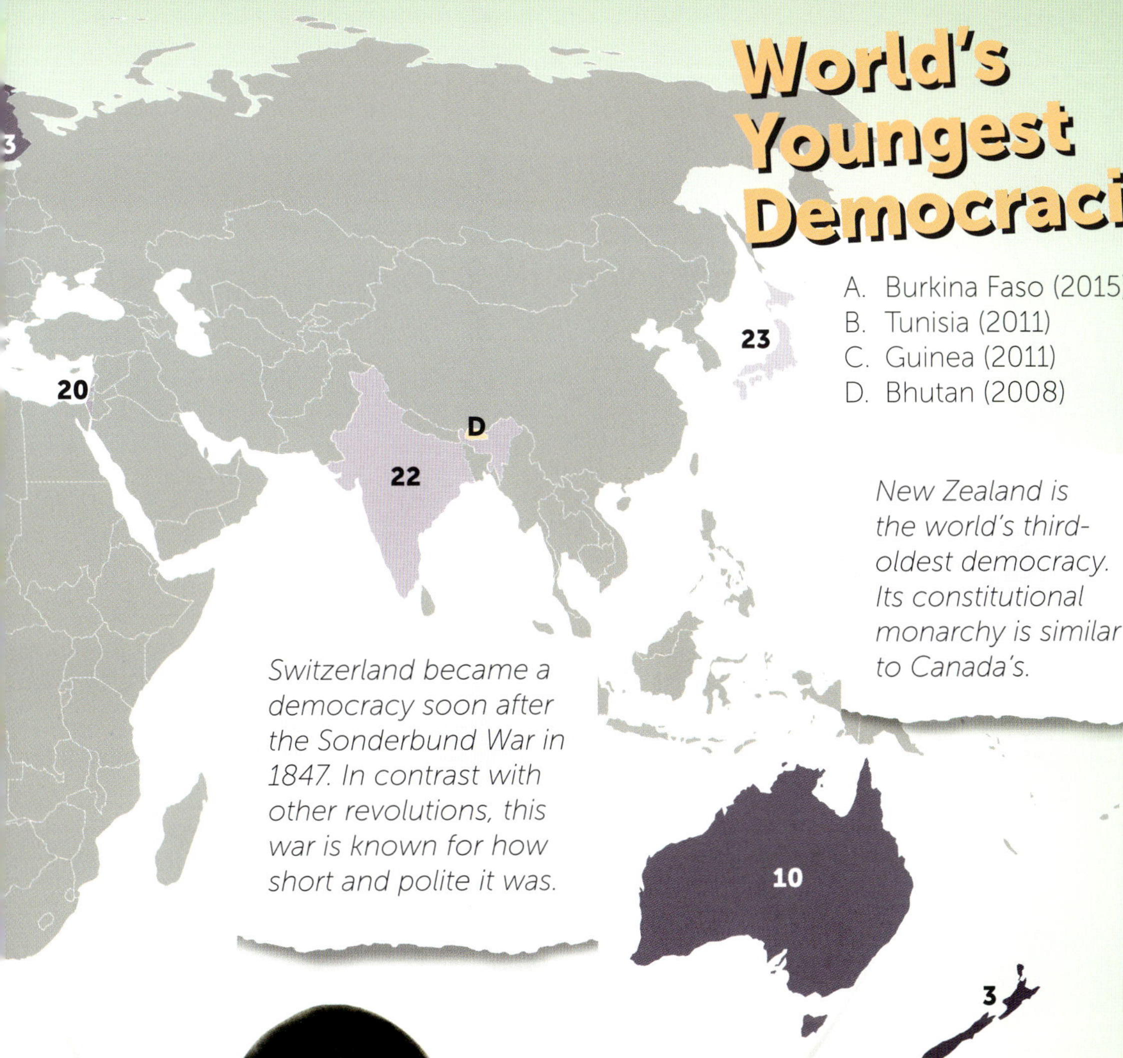

New Zealand is the world's third-oldest democracy. Its constitutional monarchy is similar to Canada's.

Switzerland became a democracy soon after the Sonderbund War in 1847. In contrast with other revolutions, this war is known for how short and polite it was.

Think About It!

Based on what you have read so far, what are some factors that can lead to the development of democracies?

CHAPTER 3

Rights For All

Today, many democratic principles are closely linked to human rights. This was not always the case.

The Americans who called for equality and freedom in the late 1700s had a narrow point of view. Much like ancient democracies in Greece and Rome, they only upheld the rights of free, male citizens. The same was true in Canada. More than half the population of North America was disenfranchised. That means they did not have the right to vote. Leaders did not represent their interests in government. They were treated like second-class citizens.

Liberal democracy has evolved over time. In 1776, when John Adams, Thomas Jefferson, Benjamin Franklin, Roger Sherman, and Robert R. Livingston presented their draft of the Declaration of Independence (shown here), they were influenced by the ideas of the time. Most of the population was not yet allowed to vote.

Ending Slavery

Slavery was abolished in Canada in 1833, when Britain ended the practice in most of its colonies. Black Canadian men got the right to vote in 1834. They had to own property, however. The property ownership rule was in place for all Canadians until 1920. In the United States, about 4 million people were enslaved before the Civil War began in 1861. President Thomas Jefferson—one of the writers of the Declaration of Independence—owned more than 600 Black people. Activists compared the way the U.S. government treated enslaved people to how Britain treated colonists. In 1862, the Emancipation Proclamation was passed to abolish slavery in the United States. The practice did not actually end until the 13th Amendment to the U.S. Constitution in 1865. American men of all races got the right to vote with the 15th Amendment in 1870. However, the constitution allowed states to control their own voting laws. Some states found ways to make it difficult for Black people to vote. Read more about the fight for civil rights on page 31.

Check It Out!

www.archives.gov/exhibits/featured-documents/emancipation-proclamation/transcript.html

The 15th Amendment stated voting rights could not be denied based on "race, color, or previous condition of servitude."

Think About It!

How might placing limits on who can vote, such as owning property, paying a poll tax**, or giving up rights, influence elections?**

The vote wasn't just given to women and minorities. They had to demand and fight for their rights.

Women's Suffrage

In the 1850s, activists organized to fight for women's **suffrage** in the United States. They argued that the 14th and 15th Amendments granted women the right to vote. It was not until 1920 that American women got the right to vote with the 19th Amendment. But the first **enfranchisements** applied only to White women. Indigenous, Black, and Asian women had to wait longer for their right to vote. In many states, laws and poll taxes had the effect of disenfranchising them, or taking away their right to vote. Voter intimidation and threats of violence also kept many from voting. The 1965 Voting Rights Act outlawed discriminatory voting practices such as literacy tests. Still, states have continued to set rules and enact laws that restrict access to voting. Federal legislators have continued to press for laws that restore equal access. In Britain's colonies in Canada, the rules for women voting depended on the location. In 1867, the BNA Act declared that only male property owners could vote. Fifty years later, White women who served in World War I, or who were related to soldiers, got the right to vote. Most White and Black Canadian women could vote the following year. Asian women and men did not have the right to vote until 1948.

14th amendment	All persons born or naturalized in the United States...are citizens... No State shall make or enforce any law which shall abridge the privileges or immunities of citizens of the United States.
15th amendment	The right of citizens of the United States to vote shall not be denied or abridged by the United States or by any State on account of race, color, or previous condition of servitude.
19th amendment	The right of citizens of the United States to vote shall not be denied or abridged by the United States or by any State on account of sex.

Suffrage for Indigenous Peoples

Millions of people already lived in North America when colonists arrived. **Treaties** that favored the American and Canadian governments took away land and rights from Indigenous peoples. Later, both the Canadian and American governments brought in laws that were meant to wipe out or **assimilate** Indigenous peoples. For example, Canada's Indian Act of 1876 forced people to give up rights from earlier agreements if they wanted to vote. In the United States, Indigenous peoples were not considered citizens until 1924. Much like the Black population, they had to fight for their right to vote from state to state. In Canada, different Indigenous peoples gained the right to vote at different times. Metis men could vote in 1867, and Metis women in 1918. First Nations men could vote in 1869, but only if they gave up their treaty rights. First Nations women and men could vote in 1960 without giving up their treaty rights. Inuit women and men could vote in 1950.

Canadian suffragists, such as Nellie McClung, fought for women's right to vote.

Anti-Asian Racism

Another group that faced racism and discrimination were people who came from East Asia. In the United States, for example, the Chinese Exclusion Act, 1882, barred people of Chinese ancestry from becoming citizens. People with East Asian ancestry would not gain the right to vote until 1952. Meanwhile, Asian Canadians were kept from voting in some provinces until 1948. This inequality and ignoring the rights of minorities was completely undemocratic.

Think About It!

People who were against voting rights for all tended to be White and wealthy. What reasons would they have to oppose it?

New Zealand is a leader in women's voting rights. Women could vote in 1893.

Universal Declaration of Human Rights

The United Nations (UN) created the Universal Declaration of Human Rights in 1948. The document was described as a Magna Carta for worldwide rights. It was written by the UN's Human Rights Commission. The declaration lists 30 human rights, which are also democratic ideals. The right to equality is central to democracy, for example. All people have equal value and should have the same opportunities. Protection against discrimination is a related human right. Other rights include the freedom to express an opinion openly and to protest peacefully. A free elementary education for every child is also a basic human right. The UN's list of rights influences social systems around the world. It is the foundation for constitutional laws and international agreements. Protecting these rights affects how a democracy runs. For instance, laws ought to apply justly to everyone, governments should be accessible and accountable to all citizens, and elections must be free and fair.

American former first lady Eleanor Roosevelt led the UN group that created the Universal Declaration of Human Rights.

Civil Rights

Both the United States and Canada had a lot of work to do to improve human rights in the 20th century. The U.S. Supreme Court had ruled that racial **segregation** was constitutional in 1896. The idea that the races were "separate but equal" was widespread. The National Association for the Advancement of Colored People (NAACP) formed in 1909. Its members fought for justice and to protect civil rights. Activists such as Dr. Martin Luther King, Jr. led protests that appealed for rights for all. It wasn't until the Civil Rights Act was passed in 1964 that discrimination was prohibited. This led the way to voting rights, improved education, and better treatment in workplaces and public spaces. It took almost 100 years—until the federal Voting Rights Act of 1965—for some Southern states to allow Black people to elect representatives. At the same time in Canada, Indigenous groups used this focus on civil rights to highlight injustices against them. One result was cultural protections added to the Canadian Charter of Rights and Freedoms in 1982.

Dr. Martin Luther King Jr.

Civil Rights marches, like this one in 1963, reminded the state and White citizens that democracy was incomplete.

CHAPTER 4

Global Overview

Places around the world took different paths as they fought for rights and independence. Some were shaped by the legacies of colonialism.

Historically, the late 1700s to mid-1800s are known as the Age of Revolutions. During that time many people became dissatisfied by how they were governed. Revolutionary movements influenced by the ideas of the Age of Enlightenment (1715–1789) and American Revolution (1765–1783) sprung up. They were revolutionized by thoughts of freedom and equality.

Casting Liberty Aside

This is seen in Latin America, for example. Spain and Portugal colonized most of the region starting in the 1500s. In the 1800s, revolutions began to spread—starting with the former French colony of Saint-Domingue (now Haiti). Most Latin American countries gained their independence from empires but not from autocracy. At independence, the principals of equality and individual rights were difficult to protect. The systems that were already in place—the ones inherited from colonial rule—usually led to military dictatorships and autocrats taking power instead of democracies. Changes in government were often the result of coups rather than elections. A coup occurs when a group takes hold of power illegally. It took until the 1980s for most of these countries to form democratic governments. However, many elected leaders slid back into authoritarian rule. Instead of serving their citizens, they abused their power.

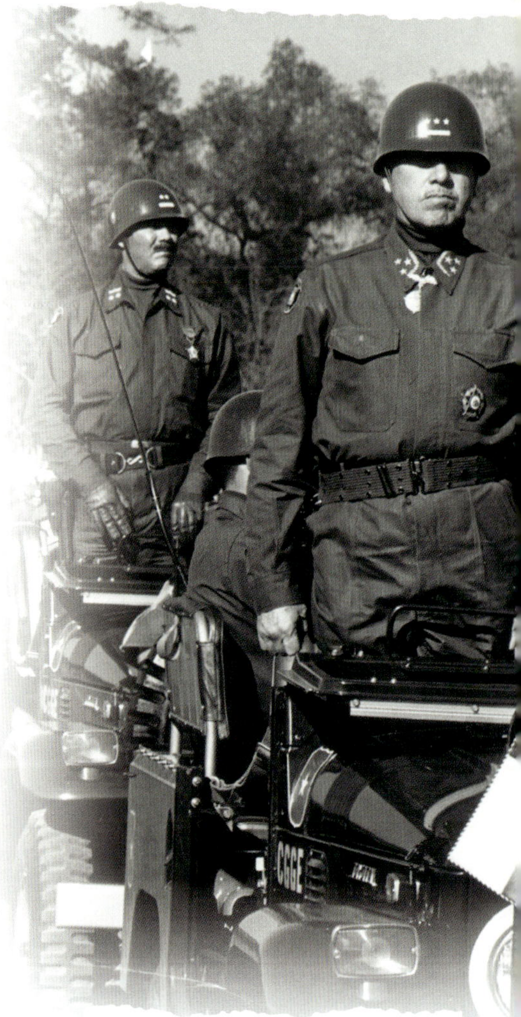

Augusto Pinochet was a general whose military dictatorship brutally ruled the South American country of Chile from 1973 to 1990.

The Mexican War of Independence was a series of revolts and events that took place over more than a decade in the early 1800s. More than 100 years later, the Mexican Revolution yet again changed the way the country was governed.

Mexican Democracy

Mexico had 300 years of colonial rule before it won its independence from Spain in 1821. During those 300 years, Spain imposed its own religion, colonial economy, and systems of rule. It was impossible to change those systems overnight. As happened in many other countries, there was a struggle for power. Conflicts and chaos—including a revolution—followed for nearly a century. In 1917, a written constitution was enacted. It has been amended hundreds of times. Mexico chose systems that were like those used in the United States. The Mexican government did not embrace democratic ideals, though. Equal treatment of all citizens was one major issue. Another problem was the lack of free and fair elections. For most of the 1900s, the Institutional Revolutionary Party was in power. People were not well represented by their government leaders. Today, Mexico is considered a flawed democracy. The same is true of over half of the countries in Latin America. Others are now autocracies. The only full democracies in the region now are Chile, Costa Rica, and Uruguay.

PRI

Think About It!

What reasons might a military have to overthrow a government?

Indian Independence and Democracy

Halfway around the world, India took another route to democracy. The British captured control of India in 1858. British colonial administrators ruled over more than 300 million Indians. For hundreds of years, Indians of all castes, or classes, and religions resisted British control and later colonial rule. Indians were forced to help fight and fund the British in World War II. Rebellions and armed resistance were common. Later, Mahatma Gandhi was one of the leaders of the Indian independence movement in its final stages. His non-violent **civil disobedience** approach was adopted as a means to force the British out. The British government finally agreed to Indian independence in 1947. Two new countries were created by dividing British India into India and Pakistan in 1947. India became a federal republic and Pakistan became a dominion and later a republic. Pakistan has some democratic and some authoritarian institutions, so it is labeled a hybrid regime. India has a president as head of state and a prime minister as the head of government. It is the world's biggest democracy. India is considered a flawed democracy because some freedoms have been lessened.

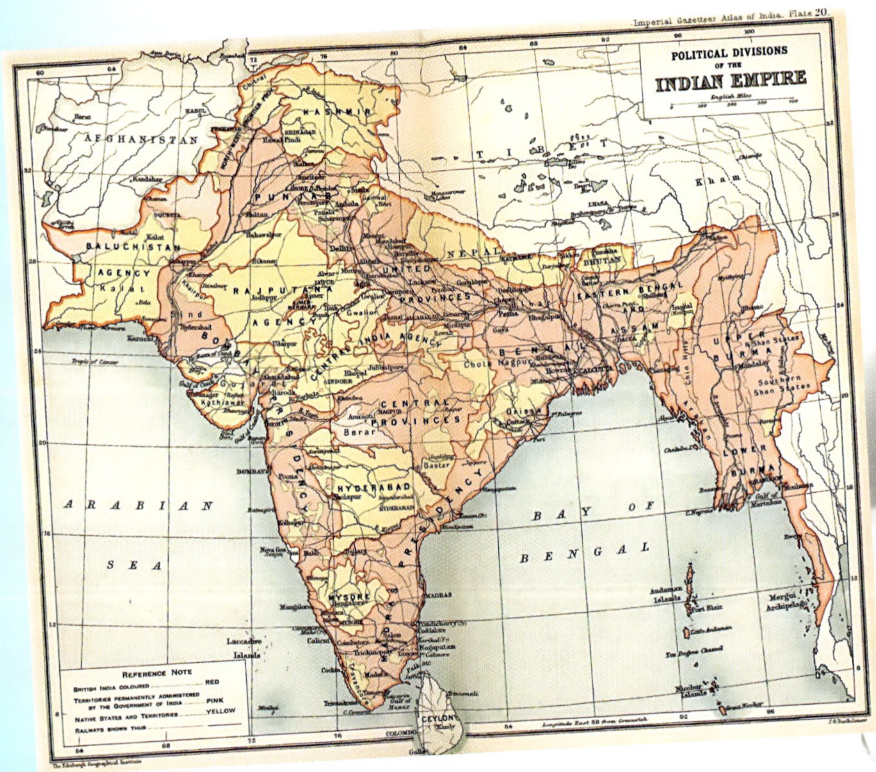

A map of British India, or the Raj, in 1909. It included enormous territory in the areas that are now India, Pakistan, Myanmar, Bangladesh, Sri Lanka, and the Maldives.

*Mahatma Gandhi's peaceful protests and **boycotts** inspired other peaceful protests.*

African Independence

Much of Africa was colonized in the 1800s. Europeans fought for control of the continent's natural resources. The competition was so fierce, it was nicknamed the Scramble for Africa. By the mid-1900s, independence movements started to form across the continent. In part, they were encouraged by India's fight for freedom. The civil rights gains made in the United States also inspired them. Activists mainly aimed for peaceful change. However, much like in Latin America, the old colonial systems that were in place led to the rise of many authoritarian governments instead of democracies.

South Africa

One of the last African countries to establish modern independence was South Africa. The former British colonies in the southernmost region of Africa formed a dominion in 1910. Similar to Canada, the Union of South Africa was a constitutional monarchy. Some citizens wanted to cut ties with Britain, though. In 1960, a referendum was held to decide on whether to become a republic. A referendum poses a single question to voters to settle a major dispute. South Africans voted to move forward without a monarch. The leaders it was left with did not represent the majority of people, however. Most South Africans were Black, but the government was run by White people. Some were the descendants of British colonists. Most were descendants of Dutch and other settlers known as Afrikaners. Their ruling political party developed a racist system called apartheid. This Afrikaans term means "aparthood" or separateness. It passed a series of laws segregating people by race and allowing legal discrimination of non-Whites.

The Pass Laws Act of 1952 required Black South Africans over 16 to carry pass books at all times.

Freedom Fighter

Nelson Mandela was a leader of the African National Congress (ANC). The ANC fought for South Africa to be a full democracy. It did this both peacefully and later through its armed wing, uMkhonto weSizwe (MK). The MK was formed by Mandela and other ANC leaders to help defend against government terror. Many ANC members were imprisoned or forced to leave South Africa for their activism. Mandela's activism often got him in legal trouble, as well. He, along with other prominent leaders of the ANC, was sentenced to prison for sabotage in 1964. It took 27 years for him to be freed. Over that time, he became an international symbol for the battle against apartheid. In the early 1990s, decades of resistance by Black and Asian South Africans and supporters, international pressure, and increasing violence, forced the South African government to realize apartheid had no future. It worked with Mandela and the ANC to end the system. South Africa's first free and fair democratic election took place in 1994. The ANC won and Mandela became the president. A new South African constitution was put in place on December 10, 1996. This is the same date that the UN marks Human Rights Day.

Nelson Mandela

The end of apartheid rule did not come without costs. Many people risked and lost their lives, just for protesting publicly.

Arab Spring

Over time and around the world, protests against leaders with absolute power have had a huge impact. They continue to this day. In December 2010, Mohamed Bouazizi set himself on fire to protest police harassment in Tunisia. This act led to protests across the country. Zine El Abidine Ben Ali had been president for 23 years. Tunisians voted him out in their first free election on October 23, 2011. Egyptians were inspired to protest, too. Their president of 30 years, Hosni Mubarak, resigned after 1 million citizens revolted against him. Soon after, protests and calls for democracy began in Bahrain, Libya, and Syria. By 2012, the fight had spread to Yemen. President Ali Abdullah Saleh was forced out after decades in power. This period of change is known as the Arab Spring. Along with protests across the Middle East and North Africa, civil wars broke out in Yemen, Syria, and Libya. Change has been slow. Time will tell whether the fights for democracy in the region will succeed.

Egyptians protest in the streets in 2013 during Arab Spring.

President Zine El Abidine Ben Ali of Tunisia was ousted in 2011 after protests against his corrupt rule.

Hosni Mubarak served as president of Egypt from 1981–2011. He was forced to step down after protests over corruption and abuse of power.

Ali Abdullah Saleh was president of North Yemen from 1978-1990, then Yemen from 1990–2012 when he was ousted during protests.

Hong Kong's Fight

Hong Kong has had a unique struggle for democracy. The British took control of the territory from China in 1841. It became an important trade link between the East and the West. In 1898, an agreement was made for Britain to keep Hong Kong until 1997. Control returned to the Chinese government that year. Over time, Hong Kong had developed a **capitalist** economy with limited democracy, but the colonial government never granted full enfranchisement. In other words, all Hong Kong citizens never had the right to directly elect their leaders. However, after 156 years of British rule, its leaders and citizens had acquired different values than the Communist Party that ruled China. With the handover to China, a new arrangement known as "one country, two systems" was established. The people living in the former British colony were promised that they would keep their rights and their **administrative** systems, and democratic reforms would continue. Since then, China has not honored its agreements with its territory. Hong Kong is in danger of losing its existing, if limited, democratic processes.

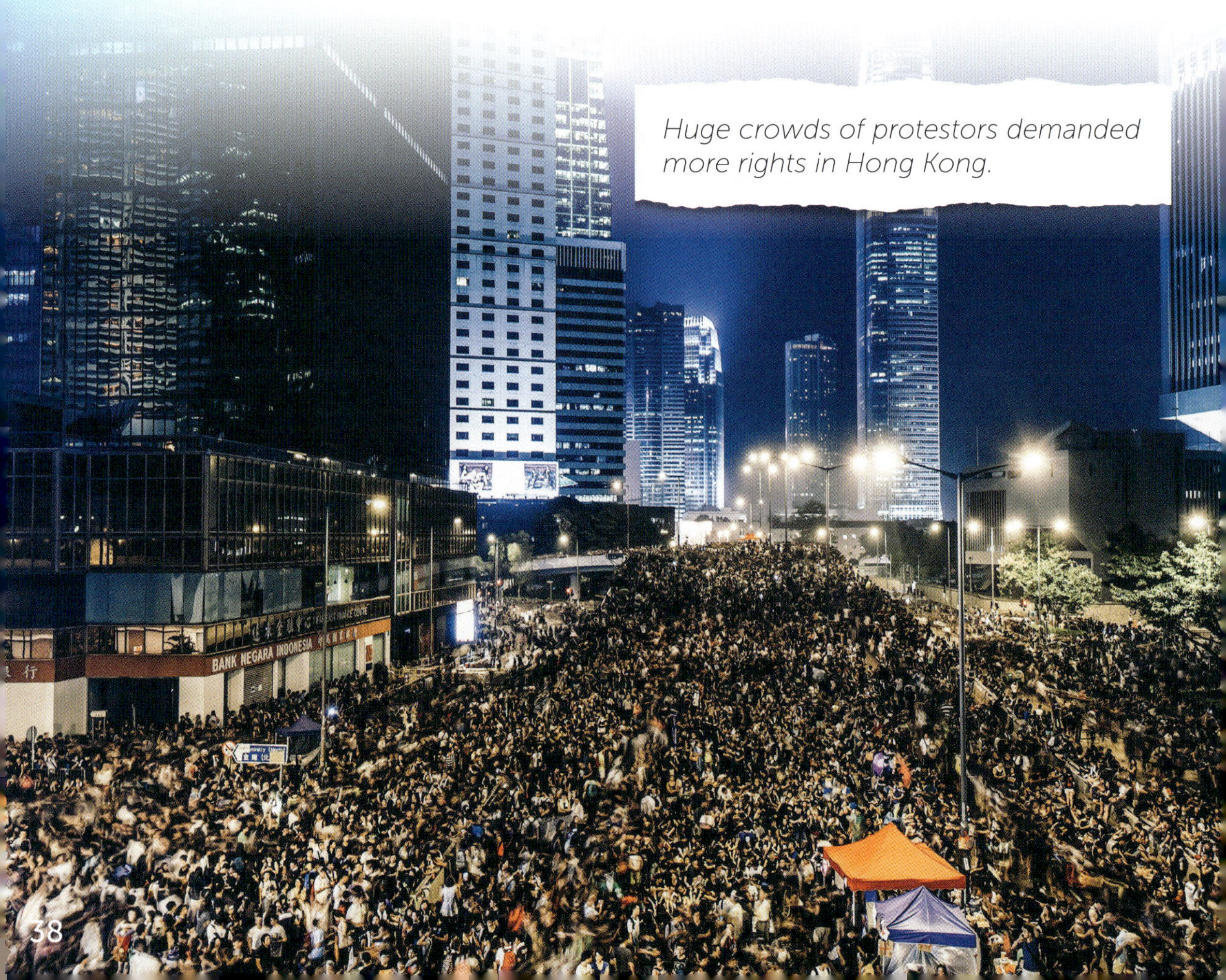

Huge crowds of protestors demanded more rights in Hong Kong.

People in Myanmar risked their lives to protest against a military coup in 2021.

Conflict in Myanmar

Democracy is fragile in many areas today. Myanmar is just one example. The country was under British rule until 1948. Gaining independence led to over a decade of political unrest. In 1962, the military took control. It took 50 years for citizens to win back their democratic government. Aung San Suu Kyi was one of the leaders of the fight. The military kept her under **house arrest** for 15 years. The National League for Democracy (NLD), led by Suu Kyi, came to power in 2015. She and her party were re-elected in February 2021. The military-backed losers demanded a new vote. Then the military, led by General Min Aung Hlaing, staged a coup. They overthrew the legal government that represented the people of Myanmar. Members of the NLD were arrested or went into hiding. Suu Kyi was put under house arrest again. The people of Myanmar continue to fight for a return to democracy. Their protests are broken up by the dictatorship's armed forces.

Aung San Suu Kyi

UN Global Goals

Solving global issues requires many countries to work together. Not all members of the United Nations are democracies. However, they do uphold the democratic ideal of furthering the common good. In 2015, the UN approved the 2030 Agenda for Sustainable Development. This action plan is intended to improve life for everyone. In particular, vulnerable people benefit from its 17 global goals. This includes children, older people, those affected by poverty, and people who live with illnesses or disabilities. Each goal includes measurable targets. For example, Goal 5 focuses on **gender equality**. It aims to end discrimination against girls and women. One of the ways this goal can be met is by having balanced numbers of women in government and other leadership roles. The UN plan helps promote democratic principles as it ensures no one is left behind.

Goal 4	Quality education for all children
Goal 10	Reduced inequalities between people living in different places and from different backgrounds
Goal 16	Peace, justice, and strong institutions

Case Study

Children's Global Vote

The World's Children's Prize program targets young people aged 10 to 18. It holds the Global Vote for the Rights of the Child each year. A group of international youth representatives chooses a list of Child Rights Heroes. These people fight for the rights of children around the world. Schools then organize their own Vote Day. Each student votes for which candidate they think should win the World's Children's Prize. The award is sometimes referred to as the Nobel Prize for children. Winners have worked in many areas, from ending child slavery to improving access to education to helping those who have special needs. Since 2000, 50 million students from 74,000 schools in 119 countries have taken part. They have learned about their rights, democracy, and the UN's Global Goals. Young people can also take part as ambassadors who inform their community about the program and children's rights. Find out more by visiting their website—the link is on page 45.

Malala Yousafzai won a Nobel Peace Prize in 2014 for her work on demanding the right to education for girls.

Check It Out!

http://www.globalgoals.org

WRAP UP

Active Citizenship

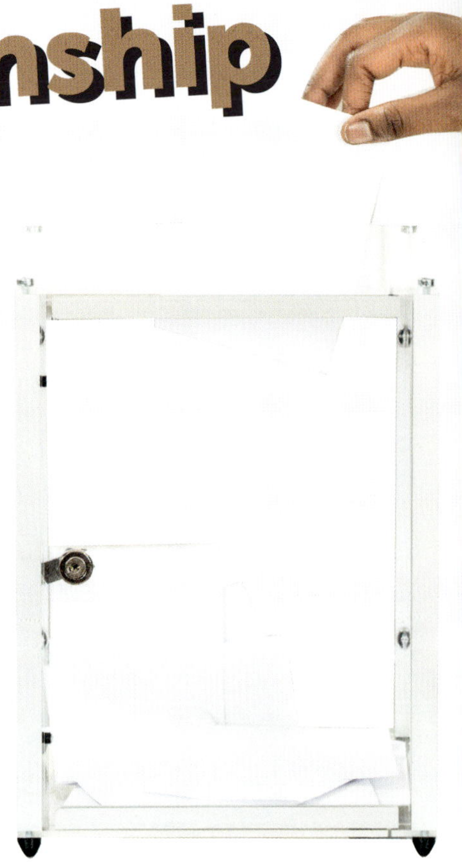

In the first American presidential election, there were very few voters and no formal political parties. George Washington was elected by huge majority over the 11 other candidates. Fast-forward to the 2020 election and about 160 million Americans went to the polls to choose between the Democrats and Republicans. It was a record high turnout—but one-third of eligible citizens did not vote. Americans went from fighting for the right to vote to not caring.

Representation Matters

Back in 1928, Canada's highest court had to decide that "persons" in the BNA Act included women. In 2015, women held half of the key leadership roles in government for the first time. When Prime Minister Justin Trudeau was asked why he pushed for this gender equality, he replied, "Because it's 2015." Change was long overdue. People from all backgrounds represent Canadians and Americans in their governments today. In 2009, Barack Obama became the first Black U.S. president. The first person of color to lead a party in Canadian parliament was Jagmeet Singh in 2017. Kamala Harris was the first female and first Asian American and Black U.S. vice president in 2021. They show the steps toward equality in countries that still struggle with discrimination.

Barack Obama

U.S. Representatives Ilhan Omar (above) and Rashida Tlaib were the first two Muslim women to serve in Congress when they were elected in 2018. Both were re-elected in 2020.

Jagmeet Singh

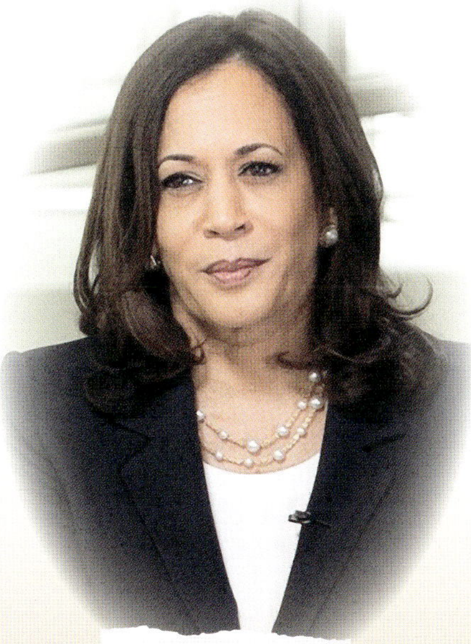

Kamala Harris

Justin Trudeau

Non-Democratic Countries Today

Some countries have never been democracies. Others have become less democratic over time. When the leaders of a country care more about themselves than they do about their citizens, it is not democratic. If basic human rights such as equality are not valued, a government does not have a foundation for democracy. Democracies also follow the rule of law, which means everyone is held equally accountable to laws. This prevents leaders from abusing their power. Without the rule of law, it is difficult for people to speak freely and make progress. Governments that do not follow the rule of law, abuse human rights, and do not represent their citizens well can still claim to be democratic. Many places use the word in their official names but are ruled by authoritarians. For example, North Korea is officially the Democratic People's Republic of Korea.

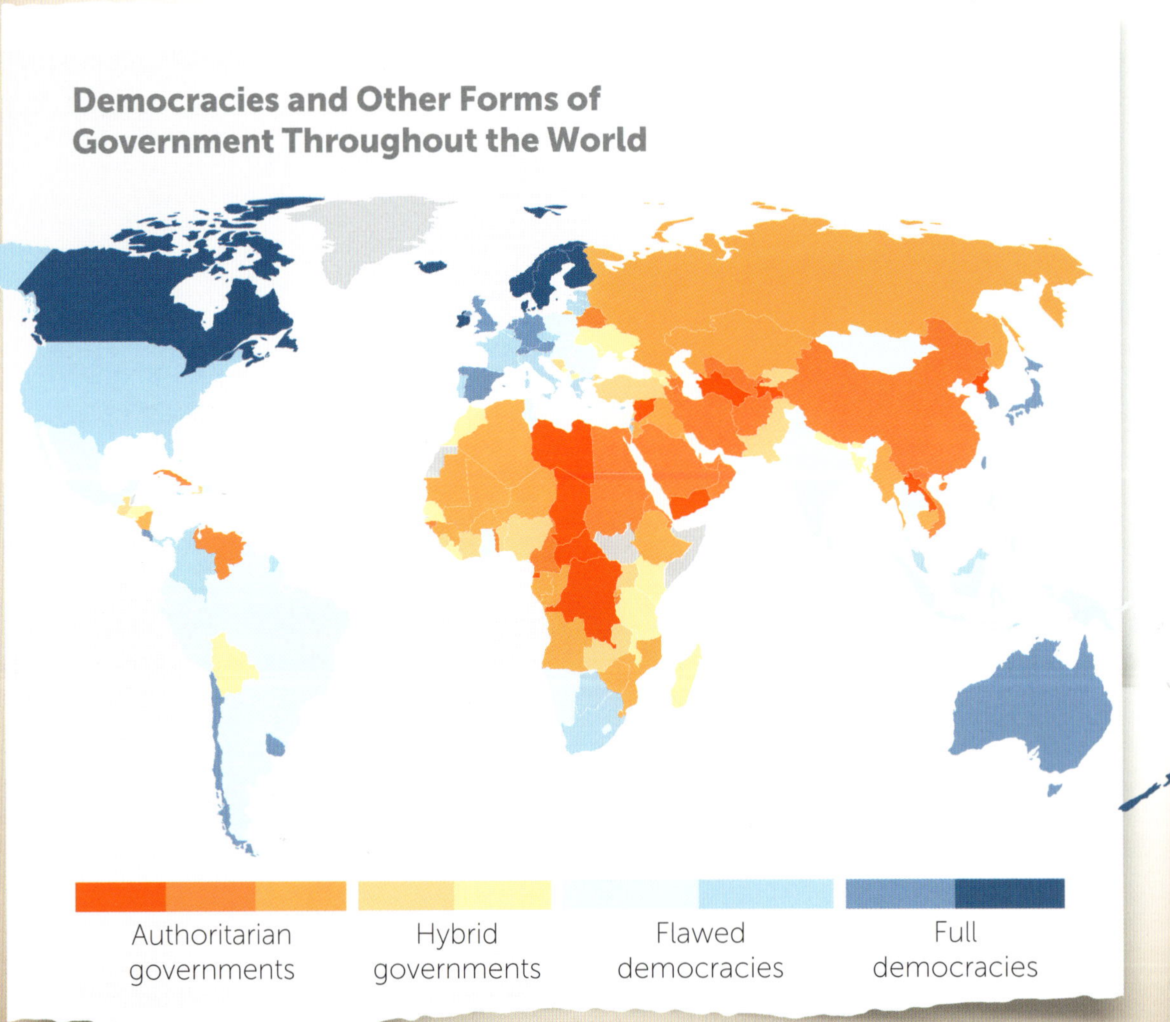

Get Involved!

Any democracy can become flawed or fail under the right conditions. These include voters not caring, political intolerance, citizens not staying informed, or politicians not being held accountable. Understanding the history of democracy and how democracies work is important to maintaining them, improving them, and making them more representative. Adults help keep their democracies healthy by voting, paying taxes, and upholding civic duties such as serving on juries. They can also form or join political parties, and even become political leaders. However, people of all ages play a role in upholding democratic values and processes. Young people can become informed about issues that affect them and their communities. They can join youth divisions of political parties. They can even help engage adults who are not doing their part. Youth can change the future for the better now!

Protesting to prompt change is another way to get involved.

Learn More

This book covers many time periods and places—and there is still plenty more to learn! Check out the resources below to dive deeper into democracy.

See the founding documents of the United States of America:	**www.archives.gov/founding-docs**
Find out more about Canadian democracy:	**https://bit.ly/3yeqMsE**
Investigate the right to vote in the United States:	**www.loc.gov/classroom-materials/elections/right-to-vote**
Explore the history of voting in Canada as told by the Canadian Museum for Human Rights:	**https://humanrights.ca/story/the-chaotic-story-of-the-right-to-vote-in-canada**
Get informed about the United Nations Global Goals for Sustainable Development:	**www.globalgoals.org**
Read more about the World's Children's Prize and the Global Vote:	**https://worldschildrensprize.org**

Bibliography

Introduction

"Citizenship Education Resources." CIVIX. civix.ca/resources

Davis, Jennifer. "The Roman Senate as Precursor of the U.S. Senate." Library of Congress. https://bit.ly/3BdRdk8

"Defining Democracy." Facing History & Ourselves. https://bit.ly/2WjTaNc

"Democracy Index 2020: In sickness and in health?" The Economist Intelligence Unit. https://bit.ly/2WtA0nT

"Greek Influence on U.S. Democracy." *National Geographic*. https://bit.ly/3yhpQDK

Heslop, D. Alan. "political system." *Britannica*. https://bit.ly/3DEQZEq

"Influence On Democracy." Haudenosaunee Confederacy. https://bit.ly/3zp2ayU

"Political system." *Science Daily*. https://bit.ly/2WqPlp7

Shvili, Jason. "What Is Authoritarian Government?" World Atlas, March 25, 2021. https://bit.ly/3gR7gwD

Chapter 1

"1866–2016: 150 Years of Democracy." Tynwald: The Parliament of the Isle of Man. https://bit.ly/2WnmVwk

"Ancient Greek Democracy." *History*, August 23, 2018. https://bit.ly/3yjhkUX

"Council of the Four Hundred." *Britannica*. https://bit.ly/3sUKiJK

"Cyrus Cylinder: How a Persian monarch inspired Jefferson." *BBC News*, March 11, 2013. https://bbc.in/3mR5sap

Edge, Peter. "1867: When democracy came to the Isle of Man." English Legal History. https://bit.ly/3A82JxB

Hofverberg, Elin. "Thingvellir—Northern Europe's First Parliament." Library of Congress, May 6, 2016. https://bit.ly/2Wmfa9F

"Magna Carta." *Britannica Kids*. https://bit.ly/2WnafWa

Desjardins, Jeff. "Mapped: The world's oldest democracies." World Economic Forum, August 8, 2019. https://bit.ly/3gyrbjE

Ninian, Arc. "Why Plato Hated Democracy." Medium. July 12, 2020. https://bit.ly/3Bf329Q

"Rome's Transition from Republic to Empire." *National Geographic*. https://bit.ly/2USHnEQ

"Two Faces of Greece: Athens & Sparta." *PBS*. https://to.pbs.org/2XY2uqr

"Your guide to the history of democracy." *History Extra*. October 30, 2020. https://bit.ly/3y3nFEk

Chapter 2

"Explore Our Country, Our Parliament." Parliament of Canada. https://bit.ly/3DlcPg2

Harris, Carolyn. "Constitutional Monarchy." *The Canadian Encyclopedia*, October 31, 2019. https://bit.ly/3ycnfLv

"How did Canada become a country?" *CBC Kids*. https://bit.ly/3kqRIAA

"King Louis XVI executed." *History*, February 4, 2021. https://bit.ly/3yd9Pi5

Lepore, Jill. "Rock, Paper, Scissors: How we used to vote." *The New Yorker*, October 6, 2008. https://bit.ly/3jeBZVS

Marks, Julie. "How Did the American Revolution Influence the French Revolution?" *History*, May 1, 2018. https://bit.ly/3x93V24

McIntosh, Andrew, and Azzi, Stephen. "Constitution Act, 1982." *The Canadian Encyclopedia*, April 24, 2020. https://bit.ly/3myOCgk

Misachi, John. "Countries With Uncodified Constitutions." World Atlas, April 25, 2017. https://bit.ly/3jgWnFN

"Our history." The Commonwealth. thecommonwealth.org/about-us/history

"parliamentary system." *Britannica*. https://bit.ly/3BAW6nz

Patrick, John. *Understanding Democracy: A Hip Pocket Guide*. New York, NY: Oxford University Press, 2006.

"Revolutionary War." *History*, December 16, 2021. https://bit.ly/2WhWDMf

"The Constitution." The White House. https://bit.ly/3zklH3d

"The Execution of Charles I." Historic Royal Palaces. https://bit.ly/3y4xbHk

"The House of Representatives." New Zealand History. https://bit.ly/3mzAXFY

"William III (r. 1689–1702) and Mary II (r. 1689–1694)." The Royal Household. www.royal.uk/william-and-mary

Chapter 3

"14th Amendment." *History*, January 12, 2021. https://bit.ly/3gxWriR

"A Brief History of Human Rights." United for Human Rights. https://bit.ly/3sKCZ76

"Black and slave population of the United States from 1790 to 1880." Statista. https://bit.ly/3sKCZE8

"Chinese Exclusion Act." *History*, September 13, 2019. https://bit.ly/3ktwMsN

Courtney, John C. "Right to Vote in Canada." *The Canadian Encyclopedia*, December 18, 2020. https://bit.ly/3BauFka

"Legal Highlight: The Civil Rights Act of 1964." U.S. Department of Labor. https://bit.ly/2WoFT5s

"Slavery at Monticello." Thomas Jefferson Monticello. www.monticello.org/slavery

Strong-Boag, Veronica. "Women's Suffrage in Canada." *The Canadian Encyclopedia*, January 28, 2021. https://bit.ly/3yvihtb

"Universal Declaration of Human Rights." United Nations. https://bit.ly/3sMOxGW

"Voting Rights for Native Americans." Library of Congress. https://bit.ly/2ThUpeb

"What Are Human Rights?" Canadian Human Rights Commission. www.chrc-ccdp.gc.ca/en

Chapter 4

"African Resistance, Nationalism and Independence." Exploring Africa. https://bit.ly/3yiBDSv

Arana, Marie. "Latin Americans Are Souring on Democracy. That's Not So Surprising Considering the Region's History." *Time*, August 27, 2019. https://bit.ly/3BsLBm4

"Biography of Nelson Mandela." Nelson Mandela Foundation. https://bit.ly/2UMjVca

Blakemore, Erin. "How Nelson Mandela fought apartheid—and why his work is not complete." *National Geographic*, July 17, 2020. https://on.natgeo.com/3y0xNxj

"Colonial Exploration and Conquest in Africa." Exploring Africa. https://bit.ly/3ks5NNY

"Democracy." United Nations. https://bit.ly/3myPfXe

"Democracy in Mexico: The Past, Present, and Future." Council on Hemispheric Affairs, July 18, 2011. https://bit.ly/3Dkg5Za

"Living in the British Empire: India." The National Archives. https://bit.ly/38b4iOy

"Mahatma Gandhi." *Biography*, September 4, 2019. https://bit.ly/3BbOZl5

"Myanmar's Aung San Suu Kyi marks third month under house arrest." *The Times of India*, May 1, 2021. http://bit.ly/3A2xLql

Pomfret, James. "Analysis: End of the road for Hong Kong's democratic dream as China 'improves' its voting system." *Reuters*, March 5, 2021. https://reut.rs/3jjyq0J

Robinson, Kali. "The Arab Spring at Ten Years: What's the Legacy of the Uprisings?" Council on Foreign Relations, December 3, 2020. https://www.cfr.org/article/arab-sping-ten-years-whats-legacy-uprisings

"The Global Vote." The World's Children's Prize. worldschildrensprize.org/theglobalvote

"Transition to Democracy: Confronting Apartheid." Facing History & Ourselves. https://bit.ly/3jjcLps

"What is the Arab Spring, and how did it start?" *Aljazeera*, December 17, 2020. https://bit.ly/3ylck1U

Wolpert, Stanley A. "British raj." *Britannica*. https://bit.ly/3gTAgUq

Yuan, Dang. "Opinion: China's autocrats end democracy in Hong Kong." DW, March 11, 2021. https://bit.ly/3zuSa6U

Wrap Up

"Barack Obama: The 44th President of the United States." The White House. https://bit.ly/3my7Gvl

Ditchburn, Jennifer. "'Because it's 2015': Trudeau forms Canada's 1st gender-balanced cabinet." *CBC*, November 4, 2015. https://bit.ly/3gt681V

"Kamala Harris: The Vice President." The White House. https://bit.ly/3yzdQOd

"United States presidential election of 1789." *Britannica*. https://bit.ly/2WKqJre

Glossary

administrative Of or related to the management of government

Age of Enlightenment A movement that influenced the way people thought about the world during the 1700s

assimilate To bring into conformity, adapt, or adjust to the rules of a dominant group of society

boycotts Refusal to have dealings with or to buy from people, organizations, or countries as a form of protest or punishment

branches Separate parts of a government

campaigners People who serve on a political, or other type, of campaign

capitalist A person or an economy that follows capitalism, an economic system and political ideology, or beliefs and ideas, based on private ownership and profit

chattel slavery Enslaving and owning humans and their offspring as property

civic duties The mandatory duties of citizens, such as obeying laws, paying taxes, and serving on juries

civil disobedience Peaceful forms of political protest such as refusing to comply with certain laws

civil war A war between citizens of the same country

class A group in a society with the same economic, cultural, or political status

corrupt Dishonest or fraudulent

enfranchisements Rights or privileges such as the right to vote

gender equality The state in which access or rights to opportunities is equal or not denied to any gender

house arrest Being held prisoner in one's own home

ideology The ideas and beliefs that inform political systems such as liberalism

jurors People who are sworn to give a verdict in a legal case

liberalism A political and social philosophy that promotes individual rights, freedoms, and democracy

majority The greater number

minority The lesser number

philosophers People who seek and study wisdom and enlightenment

poll tax A tax on every adult that does not account for income or their ability to pay

radical New and often extreme change

republic A state or country where supreme power is held by the people and not a monarch

rights Legal and social freedoms people are entitled to in a democratic society

segregation The enforced separation of different racial groups

senate A government assembly that has the power to make laws or in some countries, review, or consider them

subjects Citizens of a state

suffrage The right to vote in political elections

taxes Money the government collects from people that is used to pay for government services such as road building

treason A betrayal of loyalty towards one's own country, especially by committing harsh acts against it

treaties Agreements between countries

Index

About the Author

Rebecca Sjonger is the author of more than 50 non-fiction books for young people. She still remembers which candidate she voted for when she cast her first ballot almost 30 years ago!